DATE			

Prairie
HABITATS

BY MIRELLA S. MILLER

Published by The Child's World®
1980 Lookout Drive • Mankato, MN 56003-1705
800-599-READ • www.childsworld.com

Acknowledgments
The Child's World®: Mary Berendes, Publishing Director
Red Line Editorial: Editorial direction
The Design Lab: Design
Amnet: Production

Photographs ©: iStockphoto/Thinkstock, cover, 1;
Eric Isselee/Shutterstock Images, back cover;
Shutterstock Images, back cover, 20–21; Digital Vision, 5;
Vitoriano Junior/Shutterstock Images, 7; Svitlana
Kazachek/Shutterstock Images, 8; Elizabeth C. Doerner/
Shutterstock Images, 11; Yuri Kravchenko/Shutterstock
Images, 12–13; Max Allen/Shutterstock Images, 14;
Steshkin Yevgeniy/Shutterstock Images, 16–17;
Henk Bentlage/Shutterstock Images, 18; Mircea
Bezergheanu/Shutterstock Images, 22

ISBN 9781623239886
LCCN 2013947272

Printed in the United States of America
Mankato, MN
December, 2013
PA02192

Table of Contents

Welcome to the Prairie!

Prairies are found across a large part of North America. They are flat and rolling grasslands. Prairies are full of life. Different grasses and other plants grow here. Prairies are also home to many animals.

Plants and animals work together to live in prairies. Tall grasses give shade to animals. Some animals produce hidden tunnels. These holes allow plant roots to receive more water.

Earth's prairies are in danger. Some human activities are bad for prairies. Many prairies are turned into farmland. This results in loss of animal life. Changes in weather are making prairies warmer. There is also less rainfall. These dangers are harmful to prairies. They also hurt the animal and plant life.

Grass covers rolling and flat prairie lands.

Where Are the World's Prairies?

Prairies are found in central North America. This area is also called the Great Plains. Ten US states make up the Great Plains. Three Canadian **provinces** are also a part. The Rocky Mountains border the Great Plains to the west. The mountains block rain to the prairies. They also stop trees from growing.

There are three types of prairie. Tallgrass prairies are the wettest. The grasses here can grow more than five feet (1.5 m) tall. Tallgrass prairies are found in the eastern Great Plains. This area is around Kansas.

The driest type of prairie is the short-grass prairie. These prairies are at the bottom of the Rocky Mountains. Grasses here do not grow taller than two feet (0.6 m).

The middle of the Great Plains is called mixed-grass prairie. These prairies are not as dry as short-grass prairies. They also are not as wet as tallgrass prairies. Some grasses in mixed-grass prairies are short. Others are tall.

Central North America is the only place with prairies.

Prairie

North America

What Do Prairies Look Like?

Prairies can be flat or rolling grasslands. Grass is the most common plant. Prairies have deep, **fertile** soil.

Very few trees grow in prairies. Trees that do grow have a hard time living. Prairie grasses have thick roots. This makes it hard for tree seeds to **sprout**. Trees also need a lot of water to live.

Prairies often have fires in the spring and fall. They start easily when it is hot outside. Fires also start when the ground is dry.

These fires are important for prairie growth and survival. New plants start to bud close to the ground. This keeps them safe from the fire burning above. Fire removes a thick layer of dead grass above the new plants. Sun and rain will reach the new plants easier.

Prairie fires are good for new plant growth.

Prairie Weather

Prairies have **moderate** weather. There is a lot of sunlight in prairies. These areas receive some rain, too. Most rainfall happens from May to July. This is when plants are growing. Prairies can be windy. There are no trees to block the wind.

Summer can be hot and humid throughout prairies. Sometimes thunderstorms or tornadoes form.

Prairies cover a lot of land in the United States and Canada. This means winter is different throughout the habitat. Southern prairies will not be as cold. Prairies farther north have freezing temperatures. It can snow in these areas.

Prairies have warm weather and sunshine during parts of the year.

Plants of the Prairie

The most common plants in prairies are grasses. This plant fits well with the surroundings. Flowers and woody plants also grow in prairies.

There are four types of prairie grass. Big bluestem grass can grow up to 6.5 feet (2 m) tall. This grass grows very thick. Little bluestem grass can grow in drier parts. It grows in small bunches. It is a yellow color. Another type of grass is Indian grass. This grass can survive in hot weather. Switchgrass also grows in bunches. This grass has curly leaves.

Many wildflowers grow in prairies. Purple coneflowers and wild sunflowers grow with the grass. These wildflowers

Sunflowers are one kind of flower that grows in prairies.

need little water to grow and live. They can also grow taller than the grass. The flowers can reach the sun faster when they are tall. Prairie flowers are important for some animals. Insects pollinate the flowers. Birds eat the seeds from the wild sunflowers.

Living in the Grass

Many kinds of animals live in prairies. They live in the tall grasses or fly high in the sky. Most prairie animals live above ground among the grasses. Some catch animals that live below ground.

The badger is one animal that can dig its way underground to find food. Badgers have long, sharp front claws. They also have back feet that look like shovels. This helps them push dirt around quickly. Badgers also have a great sense of smell. They use this to find their prey.

Another animal living in the tallgrass prairies is the bull snake. This snake catches mice, birds, and squirrels. It travels below ground to find its food. Bull snakes are not poisonous. They squeeze their food before eating it. This makes sure the animal is dead.

The most famous prairie animal is the bison. Bison travel across prairies eating grass. In parts with thick grass, bison help keep the grass shorter. Grass does not overgrow in spaces that bison **graze**. Bison keep prairies healthy in other ways, too. They like to roll in the dusty ground to keep bugs away. Rolling around causes the grass to die. It also creates a hole. When it rains, this becomes a watering hole for animals.

A badger's sharp claws help it dig holes in the prairie ground.

Living Underground

Many prairie animals also live underground. One of the busiest underground animals is the earthworm. Earthworms eat dead material. Then they turn it into food for plants. Earthworms also help move deeper soil to the surface. Air and rain move through the soil easier through earthworms' tunnels. All of these activities help make prairie soil better.

There are also bigger animals that live below ground in prairies. Ground squirrels spend most of their life below ground. The prairie grass hides the opening to these squirrels' homes. The squirrels will come above ground when they need to eat.

Earthworms are busy underground animals.

The plains pocket gopher also lives below ground. This animal can find all of its food here, too. It eats the roots of plants. These gophers create mazes of tunnels using their front teeth and long claws.

The Amazing Prairie Dog

Prairie dogs are small like rabbits. These amazing animals create tunnels and towns below ground. This helps keep them safe from **predators**. A prairie dog's below-ground below ground home even has rooms! They create sleeping rooms and bathrooms.

Prairie dogs live with their families. Sometimes they live with other prairie dog families, too. Prairie dogs work together to live. They find food together and clean each other. They also team up to chase away other prairie dogs. Some prairie dogs hibernate during the winter. They survive by burning fat they stored during the warm months.

Prairie dogs spend most of their days building new tunnels and rebuilding old ones. Prairie dogs come up to eat grasses and other plants. They are careful to listen and look for predators. If a prairie dog sees danger, it makes a warning cry. This tells other prairie dogs to go below ground. A second cry means it is safe again.

Prairie dogs live together in groups and take care of each other.

Threats to the Prairie

There are many different threats to prairies. The biggest threat is farming. Prairies have ideal land for **agriculture**. The weather is moderate. There are no trees to remove, and the soil is firm. But farming leads to loss of animal life. It also means less prairie land to **preserve** as a natural habitat.

Another problem is pollution. Litter left by humans can pollute prairies. Pollution also comes from cars and farming equipment. Chemicals used by farmers are harmful to prairie plants and animals. Pollution kills plants and animals in prairies. Animals can get caught in or choke on waste.

Weather changes are also a big problem. As Earth warms up, it

Farming is a big threat to prairie habitats.

can affect weather patterns. Prairies do not receive a lot of rain. Changes in weather could mean prairies receive even less rain. Prairie plants and animals rely on the rainfall to survive. This could be dangerous for prairie life. Humans must take care of prairies so they will be a safe habitat for the plants and animals that live there.

GLOSSARY

agriculture (AG-ruh-kul-chur) Agriculture is the job of taking care of the soil, producing crops, and raising livestock. Prairies are great for agriculture.

fertile (FUR-tuhl) Fertile means to produce plenty of crops. Prairie soil is fertile and good for growing crops.

graze (GRAYZ) To graze is to feed on growing grass. Bison graze on prairie grass.

moderate (MOD-ur-it) Moderate is avoiding extremes. Prairies have moderate weather and temperatures.

predators (PRED-uh-tors) Predators live by killing and eating other animals. Prairie dogs live below ground to stay safe from predators.

preserve (pri-ZURV) To preserve is to protect. It is important for humans to preserve prairies.

provinces (PROV-uhnss-es) Provinces are large divisions of a country with their own governments. Three Canadian provinces are part of the Great Plains.

sprout (SPROUT) To sprout is to grow up. Tree seeds cannot sprout easily in prairies.

TO LEARN MORE

BOOKS

Endres, Hollie. *Prairies*. Minneapolis: Bellwether, 2008.

George, Lynn. *Prairie Dogs: Tunnel Diggers*. New York: Rosen, 2011.

Magby, Meryl. *American Bison*. New York: Rosen, 2012.

WEB SITES

Visit our Web site for links about prairie habitats:
childsworld.com/links

Note to Parents, Teachers, and Librarians: We routinely verify our Web links to make sure they are safe and active sites. So encourage your readers to check them out!

INDEX

ABOUT THE AUTHOR

Mirella S. Miller lives in Minnesota. She lives near the prairies of the Great Plains.